The Best Skillet Recipes For the Old Soul in You!

The Great Skillet Cookbook

GW00472201

Table of Contents

Introduction *4*

*Skillet Breakfasts – They'll make you look forward to
getting up!*...*7*

  1 – Farmer's Skillet Breakfast 8

  2 – Skillet Potato, Egg Sausage Breakfast....................10

  3 – French Toast Skillet.....................................13

  4 – German Skillet Pancake...............................16

  5 – Cheese Spinach Breakfast Skillet 18

Skillet-Friendly Entrees, Sides and Appetizers..................*21*

  6 – Spaghetti-Taco Skillet 22

  7 – Mediterranean Skillet Chicken 24

  8 – Kale Sweet Potato Skillet Frittata......................27

  9 – Broccoli Chicken Skillet..................................30

  10 – Skillet Tortellini Lasagna 32

  11– Beef Ramen Skillet Dinner 34

  12 – Turkey Parmesan Skillet Pasta 37

  13 – Chicken Skillet Pot Pie 40

14 – Easy Skillet Cabbage Rolls......................43

15 – Cinnamon Apple Skillet Pork Chops.....................45

16 – BLT Skillet Pasta......................49

17 – Spinach Mushroom Skillet Lasagna.....................51

18 – Skillet Sausage Cheese Pasta......................54

19 – Skillet Chili Mac......................56

20 – Spicy Chicken Ranch Skillet......................59

21 – Shrimp Skillet Tacos......................62

22 – Pasta Cheeseburger Skillet......................64

23 – Garlic Honey Skillet Chicken......................66

24 – Tater Tot Sloppy Joe Skillet Casserole.................69

25 – Pineapple-Shrimp Quinoa Skillet.........................72

Skillet Desserts... Wait 'til you try them! Yum!.................75

26 – Peach Cobbler, Skillet-Style......................76

27 – Pineapple Upside-Down Skillet Cake.................79

28 – Skillet Brownies......................82

29 – Skillet Apple Pie......................85

30 – Skillet Berry Cake......................88

Introduction

Every recipe book written on Skillet cooking would surely intimate you with amazing skillet recipes that would blow your palates away.

But what they always tend to do is to forget to teach you a few things about cooking with your cast iron skillet.

Giving you mind-blowing recipes is good but not enough. Helping you get the best of skillet cooking via important tips is more than enough.

Hence, I'd take time to brush through a few guiding tips that would help you get the best of skillet cooking.

So, here you go, skillet cooking tips for a wonderful cooking.

1. Preheat your skillet by setting it to five minutes over low heat before you start cooking.
2. Dry out your skillet immediately after washing post cooking. This is to ensure that your skillet doesn't get rusted quickly.
3. If you are cooking with a skillet for the very first time, conduct a seasoning process before anything. This seasoning process involves that you bake the skillet in oil for a few minutes, wipe it and start cooking. This baking process prevents rusting and sticking
4. Ensure that you reduce the use of acidic food items such as vinegar, citrus fruits, and tomato sauces. Concurrent use of these items, most especially in a

large quantity, in your skillet will affect your seasoning process.

5. Lastly, it is imperative that you cook with your skillet as many times as possible. As this would make you skillet last longer!!

With these tips, you would definitely enjoy cooking with your skillet!

Now, let us get to the nitty-gritty of the day, let me introduce you to amazing skillet recipes that would have you loving the "old cooking crow!!!"

Skillet Breakfasts – They'll make you look forward to getting up!

1 – Farmer's Skillet Breakfast

Makes 6-8 Servings

Cooking + Prep Time: 25 minutes

Ingredient List:

- 1/2 cup of cream, heavy
- 1/2 diced bell pepper each, one green, one red, medium
- 1 x 20-ounce pkg. of hash browns, shredded, refrigerated
- 12 eggs, large
- Seasoned salt, as desired
- 4 sliced green onions

- Pepper, black, as desired
- 1 1/2 cup of cheddar cheese shreds
- 8 ounces of cooked sausage or cubed ham
- 1/2 pound of bacon

Method:

a) Preheat oven to 350F.

b) Cook bacon in skillet till it is crisp. Remove bacon from skillet and drain on paper towels. Reserve drippings in pan.

c) Add sliced peppers and green onions to drippings. Reserve a bit of green onions to garnish.

d) Sauté mixture on med-high for three minutes, till it softens. Season using seasoning salt and pepper, as desired. Serve.

2 – Skillet Potato, Egg Sausage Breakfast

Makes 4-6 Servings

Cooking + Prep Time: 45 minutes

Ingredient List:

- 1 minced onion, yellow, medium
- 1/2 tbsp. of butter to dot top + extra for buttering the dish
- 1/4 tsp. of salt, kosher
- 4 eggs, large
- 1 cup of Colby Jack cheese, grated

- 1/4 cup of whipping cream
- 2 potatoes, medium
- 2 tbsp. of parsley, minced
- 1/2 pound of Italian sausage, ground

Method:

a) Sauté sausage in skillet. You won't need to add any oil, since it Makesits own.

b) When sausage has cooked nearly through, add the minced onion. Continue to cook while occasionally stirring, till the sausage is browned lightly and the onions have softened. Remove from the heat and allow to cool a bit.

c) Whisk together the eggs, whipping cream, 1/2 cup of cheese, salt and parsley in large bowl. Blend in sautéed sausage and the onions.

d) Peel the potatoes. Grate them. Squeeze out excess water, if any, from the potatoes. Add them to egg mixture while stirring to combine well.

e) Butter a casserole dish generously. Pour mixture into it.

f) Sprinkle top with the other 1/2 cup of cheese. Dot top with 1/2 tsp. butter. Leave dish uncovered while you bake in middle of oven for 30 to 35 minutes at

375F. Top should be golden brown. Remove from oven. Serve.

3 – French Toast Skillet

Makes 6-8 Servings

Cooking + Prep Time: 1 hour and 50 minutes plus 1/2 hour setting time

Ingredient List:

- 8 torn croissants in 2" pieces
- Optional: powdered sugar
- 1/2 cup of pecans, chopped
- 8 egg yolks from large eggs
- 1/4 tsp. of salt, kosher
- 1/4 cup of syrup, maple
- 1/2 cup of raspberries

- 1 tbsp. of vanilla extract, pure
- 1 cup of fruit preserves
- 3 cups of milk, whole

Method:

a) Preheat the oven to 350F.

b) Combine egg yolks, milk, salt, syrup and vanilla in large sized bowl. Whisk the mixture until it is frothy.

c) Heat preserves in small pan till warm and easily poured.

d) Arrange 1/2 croissant pieces in bottom of skillet. Drizzle using 1/2 of the warmed preserves. Pour 1/2 of egg mixture over croissants.

e) Repeat this step with the rest of the croissant pieces, egg mixture and preserves.

f) Press croissants lightly with spoon to aid in saturating with the fluid. Do not allow to become completely submerged. Set aside for about 1/2 hour before you bake.

g) Sprinkle casserole with raspberries and pecans. Cover skillet with foil. Bake for 1/2 hour. Remove foil. Continue to cook till golden and puffed.

h) Allow to set for 12-15 minutes. Garnish with powdered sugar, if you like. Serve at room temperature or warm.

4 – Cheese Spinach Breakfast Skillet

Makes 1-2 Servings

Cooking + Prep Time: 1/2 hour

Ingredient List:

- 1/8 tsp. of salt, kosher
- 1 small potato, russet, with skin on
- Pepper, freshly ground
- 1 slice of bacon
- 1 tbsp. of oil, olive
- 3 cups of spinach, baby
- 1 1/2 oz. of cheddar cheese shreds
- 2 eggs, large

Method:

a) Prick the potato in a few spots using a fork, and microwave on the High setting for three or four minutes. Allow to cool for about five minutes. Chop into cubes of about 1/2" each.

b) Cook the bacon on med-high in cast-iron skillet, just until it is crisp. Remove from skillet but leave drippings.

c) Add cubed potatoes and oil. Stir frequently while cooking until potatoes have browned. This takes five minutes or so.

d) Add the spinach. Stir and combine until it barely wilts. Add salt to season.

e) Use a spoon to create two wells in center of hash. Crack one egg in per well. Lower heat to med. Cook for two or three minutes, till eggs set partially. Sprinkle the cheese on top.

f) Cover. Cook till egg whites have fully set and cheese has melted. Chop bacon. Sprinkle it on the top. Garnish with pepper grinding. Serve.

5 – German Skillet Pancake

Makes 1-3 Servings

Cooking + Prep Time: 20 minutes

Ingredient List:

- 3 tbsp. of butter, melted
- 1/2 cup of flour, all-purpose
- 1 tbsp. of sugar, granulated

- 3 eggs, large
- 1/4 tsp. of salt, kosher
- 1/2 cup of milk, 2%

Method:

a) Preheat the oven to 450F.

b) Whisk eggs, sugar, salt, butter and milk in medium bowl. Add flour. Stir till combined well, but don't overmix.

c) Add 1 tbsp. of melted butter to skillet. Pour the batter in. Bake for 13-20 minutes. Edges should be starting to brown. Add your toppings. Remove from oven. Serve.

Skillet-Friendly Entrees, Sides and Appetizers

6 – Spaghetti-Taco Skillet

Makes 6 Servings

Cooking + Prep Time: 35 minutes

Ingredient List:

- 1 x 1 1/2-ounce pkg. of taco seasoning mix, mild
- 6 tbsp. of sour cream, reduced fat
- 1 x 10-ounce can of diced tomatoes with green chilies, including juices
- 1 lb. of ground beef, extra lean
- 8 oz. of uncooked spaghetti
- 2 1/2 cups of water, filtered

Method:

a) Cook and stir the beef in a large sized skillet on med-high for seven minutes. Meat should be well-crumbled with no remaining pink.

b) Add the tomatoes with juice and taco seasoning. Combine by stirring.

c) Break the spaghetti in half. Add to skillet. Bring to boil. Cover and reduce the heat. Cook while stirring for 10 minutes. Spaghetti should be tender.

d) Top with sour cream and serve.

7 – Mediterranean Skillet Chicken

Makes 4 Servings

Cooking + Prep Time: 25 minutes

Ingredient List:

- 1 tbsp. of oregano, dried
- Olive oil, as needed

- 1 1/2 cup of diced tomatoes, small
- 1/2 cup of chicken broth, low sodium
- 4 chicken breasts, skinless, boneless
- 1/4 cup of green olives, sliced
- 1/2 cup of white wine, dry
- Feta cheese, crumbled
- 1 lemon, juice only
- 1 cup of red onion, chopped finely
- Black pepper, ground
- Salt, kosher
- 2 tbsp. of garlic, minced
- 1 handful chopped parsley, fresh, with removed stems

Method:

a) Pat chicken dry. Make three slits on each side of chicken breasts, going through.
b) Spread the minced garlic onto both sides of chicken. Insert some of the garlic in the slits made in step 1.
c) Season chicken breasts with salt, ground pepper and 1/2 dried oregano on both sides.

d) Heat 2 tbsp. of oil over med-high heat in large, heavy skillet. Place chicken in skillet and brown the breasts on each side.

e) Add white wine. Allow to reduce by about a half. Add chicken broth and lemon juice. Sprinkle the rest of the oregano over the top. Lower heat to med-low.

f) Cover skillet. Cook for 10 to 15 minutes. Turn chicken once. Chicken is cooked through when its internal temperature is 170F.

g) Uncover skillet. Top with olives, onions and tomatoes. Re-cover. Cook for three more minutes.

h) Add feta cheese and parsley. Serve. It goes well with couscous, pasta or rice.

8 – Kale Sweet Potato Skillet Frittata

Makes 4 Servings

Cooking + Prep Time: 35 minutes

Ingredient List:

- 3 ounces of goat cheese
- 2 garlic cloves
- 1 cup of half 'n half

- 6 eggs, large
- 1/2 red onion, small
- 2 cups of chopped, packed kale
- 2 tbsp. of oil, olive
- 2 cups of sweet potatoes
- 1 tsp. of salt, kosher
- 1/2 tsp. of pepper, ground

Method:

a) Preheat the oven to 350F. Whisk together the eggs, half 'n half, salt ground pepper.

b) Sauté the sweet potatoes in a tbsp. of hot oil in oven-proof skillet on med. heat for eight to 10 minutes. Sweet potatoes should be golden in color and tender. Remove the potatoes and keep them warm.

c) Sauté the kale, garlic and onion in the last 1 tbsp. of oil for several minutes, till kale is tender and wilted. Add sweet potatoes while stirring.

d) Pour the egg mixture over vegetables evenly. Cook for a few more minutes. Sprinkle the goat cheese into the egg mixture.

e) Bake for 10-15 minutes in 350F oven, till mixture sets. Remove from oven. Serve.

9 – Broccoli Chicken Skillet

Makes 4-6 Servings

Cooking + Prep Time: 45 minutes

Ingredient List:

- 1 to 2 cups of chicken, cooked (use canned chicken if you don't have time to cook it)
- 1 cup of cashews
- 2 tbsp. of soy sauce
- 2 tbsp. of cornstarch dissolved in 1/4 cup water, filtered

- 1/2 cup of yellow onion, sliced
- 1 1/2 cup of chicken stock
- 1 tbsp. of oil, olive
- 1/4 cup of sugar, brown
- 4 cups of broccoli, raw
- 2 minced garlic cloves

Method:

a) Add the chicken stock, oil, soy sauce, sugar, garlic, chicken, onion, cashews and broccoli to large sized skillet. Heat over high. Cover and bring to boil.

b) When ingredients are boiling, lower heat to med. Allow to boil for seven to eight minutes. Broccoli should be tender.

c) When broccoli has cooked through, add the cornstarch/water mix to thicken sauce. Stir well.

d) Remove skillet from the heat. Serve over rice.

10 – Skillet Tortellini Lasagna

Makes 6 Servings

Cooking + Prep Time: 1/2 hour

Ingredient List:

- 24 oz. of spaghetti sauce
- 2 cups of mozzarella cheese shreds
- 1 x 20-oz. pkg. of cheese tortellini, refrigerated
- 1 tsp. of Italian seasoning

- Optional: 1/2 tsp red pepper, crushed, if you like spicy dishes
- 1 pound of beef, ground

Method:

a) Brown beef in large sized skillet on med. heat. Sprinkle using Italian seasoning.

b) Add and stir spaghetti sauce. Add red pepper flakes, as desired. Add tortellini. Simmer for about five minutes.

c) Sprinkle mozzarella over top of tortellini evenly. Cover. Cook for three to five minutes. Cheese should be fully melted. Remove from heat. Serve hot.

11– Beef Ramen Skillet Dinner

Makes 6 Servings

Cooking + Prep Time: 40 minutes

Ingredient List:

- 1 broccoli head, sliced in florets
- 1 tbsp. of oil, olive
- 1/2 tsp. of sesame seeds
- 1 lb. of sliced flank steak

- 2 x 5.6-ounce pkgs. of Yaki-Soba refrigerated ramen noodles w/discarded seasoning packets (found in refrigerated aisles of grocery stores)

For sauce

- 1/4 cup of honey, pure
- 3 tbsp. of vinegar, rice wine
- 1 tbsp. of oil, sesame
- 3 tbsp. of packed brown sugar
- 1 tbsp. of corn starch
- 3/4 cup of broth, beef
- Optional: 1 tsp. of sriracha, for extra spiciness
- 3/4 cup of soy sauce, reduced sodium
- 1 tbsp. of ginger, grated
- 4 minced garlic cloves

Method:

a) Whisk 1/2 cup of filtered water, soy sauce, ginger, corn starch, sesame oil, garlic, brown sugar, vinegar, honey, beef broth and sriracha (if using) together in medium-sized bowl. Set the bowl aside.

b) In large sized pot 1/2-filled with boiling water, add the Yaki-Soba noodles until they become loosened. Drain them well.

c) Heat the oil in large sized skillet on med-high. Add the steak. Cook and flip once, till it has browned.

d) Stir in the Yaki-Soba, soy sauce mixture and broccoli, till broccoli becomes tender and sauce becomes a bit thicker.

e) Sprinkle sesame seeds on top, as desired. Serve promptly.

12 – Turkey Parmesan Skillet Pasta

Makes 6 Servings

Cooking + Prep Time: 1/2 hour

Ingredient List:

- 3/4 cup of Parmesan cheese
- 1 diced green pepper
- 1 diced onion
- 2 cups of beef broth, low sodium
- 2 cups of pasta, whole wheat, uncooked

- 1 can of tomatoes, diced, with Italian spices
- 1 pound of turkey, ground

Method:

a) Sauté green pepper and onions till they soften, in large sized skillet on med-high.

b) Add ground turkey. Break it into small sized pieces as it cooks. Once done, remove it from the pan into bowl. Leave the juice and drippings in the pan. Set meat mixture bowl aside.

c) Return skillet to heat. Add pasta, beef broth and tomatoes. Stir and coat pasta. Bring to boil before reducing the heat to med.

d) Cover. Cook for 12-15 minutes. Pasta should be tender.

e) Return the vegetable-turkey mix to skillet. Add in 1/2 cup of cheese while stirring. Heat mixture completely through. Sprinkle with Parmesan cheese. Serve.

13 – Chicken Skillet Pot Pie

Makes 8 Servings

Cooking + Prep Time: 1 1/2 hours

Ingredient List:

- 3 tbsp. of cream, heavy
- 1 egg, large
- 1 pre-made pie crust
- 1/2 tsp. of salt, kosher
- 4 carrots, medium
- 1 onion, medium
- 1 cup of peas, frozen
- 2 garlic cloves

- 2 tbsp. of butter, unsalted
- 1/2 tsp. of pepper, ground
- 4 cups of cooked chicken, shredded
- 2 tbsp. of flour, all-purpose
- 2 cups of broth, chicken
- 1 1/2 tbsp. of fresh dill, chopped
- 2 celery stalks

Method:

a) Preheat the oven to 400F. Heat the butter in skillet on med. heat.

b) Add the garlic, celery, carrots and onion. Cook till carrots have started softening. Seasoning using kosher salt and ground pepper.

c) Reduce the heat to med-low. Add flour while stirring. Cook for a minute.

d) Add broth and cream and combine with a whisk. Stir in the dill, chicken and peas. Bring them to boil. Remove from the heat.

e) Roll pie crust out till it is 12" diameter. Place dough on top of the chicken mixture. Brush with the egg. Cut small vents in the top of the pastry.

f) Transfer the skillet into the oven. Bake till crust becomes flaky and brown. This usually takes a half-hour to 35 minutes. Remove from oven. Allow to cool a bit and serve.

14 – Easy Skillet Cabbage Rolls

Makes 6 Servings

Cooking + Prep Time: 55 minutes

Ingredient List:

- 1 tsp. of oregano
- Basil, chopped, if desired
- A pinch of fresh thyme
- 2 pinches hot pepper flakes, if you desire a spicy dish

- 2 1/2 cups of water, filtered
- 1 tbsp. of oil, olive
- 3/4 cup of rice, uncooked
- 1/2 tsp. of salt, kosher
- 1 lb. of ground beef, lean
- 1 can of chopped plum tomatoes, with no spices, etc., added
- 1 chopped garlic clove
- 4 cups of cabbage, chopped
- 1/2 chopped onion, yellow

Method:

a) Add ground beef, oil, onion and garlic to large skillet. Cook over med. heat till they have browned.

b) Add remainder of ingredients. Combine by stirring. Cover the skillet and cook on med-low for about 1/2 hour, till thickened and cooked through. Serve.

15 – Cinnamon Apple Skillet Pork Chops

Makes 2 Servings

Cooking + Prep Time: 1/2 hour

Ingredient List:

- 4 chopped apples, tart, medium
- 3 tbsp. of sugar, brown
- 1/2 tsp. of nutmeg, ground
- 1/2 tsp. of salt, kosher
- 4 tbsp. of butter, unsalted

- 1 tsp. of pepper, black
- 1 tsp. of cinnamon, ground
- 2 pork chops, bone-in

For sweet potatoes:

- 1/2 tsp. of cinnamon, ground
- 4 tbsp. of butter, unsalted
- 1 tbsp. of sugar, brown
- Salt, kosher
- 3/4 cup of cream, heavy
- 6 peeled, cubed sweet potatoes

For garnishing:

- Rosemary, fresh

Method:

a) Bring large pot with lightly salted, filtered water to boil. Add the potatoes. Cook for 20-30 minutes till they are tender.

b) Mix 1 tsp. pepper, salt and 1 tbsp. of brown sugar together in small sized bowl. Season pork chops with this mixture. Set aside.

c) Heat 2 tbsp. of butter on med. heat in large skillet. Add the pork chops. Cook for three to five minutes per side.

d) Remove pork chops. Set them aside, keeping them warm.

e) Add cinnamon, nutmeg, 2 tbsp. of brown sugar, chopped apples and last 2 tbsp. of unsalted butter to skillet.

f) Stir and cook till the apples become tender. This usually takes between seven and 10 minutes.

For the mashed sweet potatoes:

g) Once potatoes have cooked, mix on low and blend the potatoes while adding the cream slowly, till you have your preferred texture. Add cinnamon, salt, brown sugar and butter as desired, and blend the potatoes till smooth.

h) Place pork chops on sweet potatoes and top with the apples. Garnish using rosemary. Serve.

16 – BLT Skillet Pasta

Makes 3 Servings

Cooking + Prep Time: 45 minutes

Ingredient List:

- 7 ounces of fettuccine, refrigerated
- 2 tbsp. of mayonnaise
- 2 tbsp. of cream, heavy
- 1 x 14 1/2 ounce can of diced tomatoes, fire roasted
- 6 to 8 bacon slices

- 2 cups of baby arugula, packed

Method:

a) Bring filtered water to boil in large pot.

b) Slice bacon in 1/2" slices. Place in skillet. Cook and stir over med. heat till bacon has cooked and has started to crisp. Strain some fat out but leave several tbsp. of fat in pan.

c) Add arugula and tomatoes with juice. Cook till arugula wilts.

d) Whisk cream and mayo together. Pour into skillet. Stir completely. Reduce the heat to low.

e) Salt the boiling water in pot. Add pasta. Only cook for three minutes. Strain pasta. Add to skillet. Cook while stirring for a couple minutes. Serve.

17 – Spinach Mushroom Skillet Lasagna

Makes 8 Servings

Cooking + Prep Time: 1 hour 40 minutes

Ingredient List:

- 2 garlic cloves
- 12 lasagna noodles, no-boil
- 8 ounces of six-cheese shredded Italian blend
- 10 ounces of alfredo sauce, light, refrigerated
- Salt, kosher

- 1 red bell pepper, small
- 1 egg, large
- 1 sweet onion, medium
- 5 ounces of kale or baby spinach
- 3 tbsp. of oil, olive
- 1/4 cup of basil, chopped
- 2 ounces of Parmesan cheese
- 16 ounces of ricotta, whole milk
- 1 can of tomatoes, diced
- 12 ounces of mushrooms, your choice of type
- Pepper, black, ground

Method:

a) Preheat the oven to 400F.

b) Stir 1/4 cup of Parmesan, 1 cup of cheese blend, egg, basil and ricotta together in a medium bowl. Season with 1/2 tsp. each of kosher salt ground pepper.

c) Heat 1 tbsp. of oil in large sized skillet on med-high. Add the mushrooms. Sauté them, occasionally stirring, till browned lightly. Remove them to a small bowl. Add 1 more tbsp. of oil to the skillet.

d) Add bell pepper and onion. Stir occasionally while sautéing them until they are tender. This usually takes between four and six minutes. Add garlic and spinach. Stir while sautéing until they are wilted.

e) Add the tomatoes and onion mixture to bowl of mushrooms. Combine well. Season using kosher salt and ground pepper.

f) Wipe the skillet clean. Coat with last tbsp. of oil. Arrange four noodles in the bottom of the skillet. Break them if needed, so they form one layer.

g) Top with 1/3 each of alfredo sauce, vegetable mixture and ricotta mixture. Repeat twice more, layering the noodles sideways to the layer below them. Top with last of Parmesan cheese and cheese blend.

h) Bake for about 1/2 hour, until lasagna is golden brown. Sprinkle with sliced basil and serve.

18 – Skillet Sausage Cheese Pasta

Makes 3-5 Servings

Cooking + Prep Time: 45 minutes

Ingredient List:

- 1 tbsp. of garlic, minced

- 1 cup of cheddar-jack cheese shreds

- 1/2 tsp. each kosher salt and ground pepper

- 8 oz. of pasta, dry

- For garnishing: 1/3 cup of scallions, chopped
- 2 cups of broth, chicken
- 1 x 10-ounce can of tomatoes, diced
- 1 cup of onion, diced
- 1 pound of sliced smoked turkey sausage
- 1 tbsp. of oil, olive
- 1/2 cup of milk, whole

Method:

a) Add the oil to skillet on med-high. Add sausage and onions. Cook till they have browned lightly. Add the garlic. Cook for 1/2 minute.

b) Add pasta, milk, tomatoes, seasonings and broth. Bring to boil. Then cover. Reduce the heat to low. Simmer for 15 minutes or so, till pasta becomes tender.

c) Turn heat off. Stir in 1/2 cup cheese. Sprinkle rest of cheese over the top. Cover for three to five minutes, so cheese can melt. Top with scallions. Serve.

19 – Skillet Chili Mac

Makes 6 Servings

Cooking + Prep Time: 45 minutes

Ingredient List:

- 1/4 tsp. each of paprika, salt (kosher) and ground pepper
- 15-ounce can of tomatoes

- Optional additions: kidney beans, bell peppers or other diced veggies
- 1 tbsp. of chili powder
- 1 yellow onion, large
- 8 ounces of macaroni
- 1 tbsp. of sugar, brown
- 2 minced garlic cloves
- 15-ounce jar of marinara sauce
- 1 tbsp. of oil, olive, for coating pan
- 1 tsp. of cumin, ground
- 1 pound of beef, ground
- 2 cups of water, filtered

Method:

a) Heat the oil in skillet over med. heat.
b) Dice the onion.
c) Place garlic and onion in skillet. Sauté till softened slightly.
d) Add the spices. Cook for about a minute, till the mixture is aromatic.
e) Add ground beef. Cook till there is no pink remaining. Break into small pieces while cooking.

f) Sprinkle with salt and brown sugar. Cook for another minute.

g) Add the water, sauce and tomatoes, then pasta. Increase the heat up to high. Bring almost to boil.

h) Reduce the heat back to low. Simmer for 18-20 minutes. All water should be absorbed, and pasta should be completely cooked.

i) Sprinkle cheese on top. Remove from heat. Serve.

20 – Spicy Chicken Ranch Skillet

Makes 2-4 Servings

Cooking + Prep Time: 50 minutes

Ingredient List:

- 1 can of diced tomatoes
- 2 cored, chopped bell peppers – 1 red, 1 green
- 1/4 chopped red or yellow onion
- 3/4 cup of chicken stock, low sodium
- 1 can of drained, rinsed black beans

- 2 tsp. of oil, olive
- 1 packet of ranch mix, spicy
- 1 1/2 cups of brown rice, instant
- 1 cup of cheddar cheese, grated
- 1 lb. of cubed chicken breasts, skinless, boneless
- To serve: cilantro

Method:

a) Heat oil in large sized skillet. Add onion. Sauté till it is translucent.

b) Add bell peppers. Cook till they have softened. Add chicken. Cook for three to five minutes.

c) Add chicken stock, brown rice, tomatoes, ranch mix and black beans. Mix well. Bring mixture to boil. Cover and reduce heat. Allow to simmer for 15-20 minutes. Rice should be tender and chicken cooked all the way through.

d) Add cheddar cheese to top of mixture. Remove from heat. Cover. Allow to set for a minute or so, allowing cheese to melt fully.

e) Add more cheese and cilantro, as desired. Serve.

21 – Shrimp Skillet Tacos

Makes 4 Servings

Cooking + Prep Time: 25 minutes

Ingredient List:

- 1/4 cup of cilantro, fresh
- 2 tbsp. of oil, canola
- 4 cups of red cabbage, sliced thinly
- 2 tbsp. of lime juice, fresh
- 2 tsp. of lime zest, grated
- 12 ounces of shrimp, small

- For serving: lime wedges, sour cream, hot pepper sauce (if desired)

Method:

a) Toss lime juice and cabbage in large bowl.
b) In another bowl, toss the lime zest and cilantro with the shrimp.
c) Heat oil over med-high heat in skillet till quite hot. Add a single layer of shrimp. Cook for about two minutes, till shrimp are opaque.
d) Add shrimp to tortillas with the cabbage mixture, lime wedges, hot pepper sauce and sour cream, as desired. Serve.

22 – Pasta Cheeseburger Skillet

Makes 6 Servings

Cooking + Prep Time: 35 minutes

Ingredient List:

- 1/2 tsp. of garlic salt

- 1 1/4 cups of water, filtered

- 1 cup of blended Monterey Jack and Cheddar cheese shreds

- 2 cups of uncooked pasta shells, medium sized
- 1/2 cup of onion, chopped
- 1 lb. of ground beef, lean
- 1 x 15-ounce can of tomato sauce
- 1/4 cup of tomato ketchup

Method:

a) Heat a large skillet on med-high. Add the onion, garlic salt and beef.

b) Cook for seven or eight minutes and crumble beef till it shows no pink. Drain well.

c) Add water, tomato sauce and pasta and combine by stirring. Bring to boil. Cover the skillet. Reduce the heat. Cook for 10-12 minutes, till pasta becomes tender.

d) Add ketchup while stirring. Top dish with cheese. Allow the skillet to sit until the cheese has melted. Serve.

23 – Garlic Honey Skillet Chicken

Makes 4 Servings

Cooking + Prep Time: 50 minutes

Ingredient List:

- 1/4 cup of soy sauce, low sodium
- To garnish: sesame seeds and green onions
- 1 tsp. of sriracha
- 2 tbsp. of oil, sesame

- 1 lime, juice only
- 1 pound of chicken breasts, skinless, boneless
- 3 tbsp. of honey, pure
- 1 tbsp. of corn starch
- 2 minced garlic cloves

Method:

a) Preheat the oven to 350F.

b) To create the glaze, whisk together the corn starch, 1 tbsp. sesame oil, sriracha, lime juice, garlic, honey and soy sauce in medium sized bowl.

c) Season the chicken using kosher salt and ground pepper.

d) In oven-proof skillet on med-high, heat the oil. Sear the chicken. Allow it to cook till it is golden. Flip. Cook for four minutes or so on other side. Pour glaze over chicken. Transfer skillet to the oven.

e) Bake till chicken has cooked completely through. This takes about 20-25 minutes. Heat the broiler.

f) Spoon the glaze over the chicken. Broil for two minutes. Use sesame seeds and green onions to garnish. Serve.

24 – Tater Tot Sloppy Joe Skillet Casserole

Makes 6 Servings

Cooking + Prep Time: 1 1/2 hours

Ingredient List:

- 2 minced garlic cloves
- 8 oz. of tomato sauce

- 1 tsp. of mustard, prepared
- 1/4 tsp. of onion powder
- 2 tbsp. of sugar, brown
- Black pepper, ground, as desired
- 1/2 cup of ketchup, low sodium
- 1 x 15-oz. can of rinsed and drained pinto beans
- 2 tbsp. of Worcestershire sauce
- 1 x 16-oz. bag of tater tots, frozen
- 1/2 tsp. of garlic powder
- 1 1/2 cups of cheddar cheese, grated
- 1 lb. of turkey or beef, ground

Method:

a) Set oven-safe, medium sized skillet on med-low. Add several drops of olive oil. Sauté garlic for one or two minutes, till very lightly browned and barely fragrant.

b) Add ground meat. Raise heat to med-high. Cook till the meat doesn't have any pink in it. Stir and break apart as it cooks. Drain grease.

c) As meat browns, place oven rack in middle position. Preheat oven to 425F.

d) To prepare sauce, combine ketchup, tomato sauce, pepper, onion and garlic powders, mustard, brown sugar and Worcestershire sauce, as desired. Pour sauce over browned meat. Combine well and mix in pinto beans.

e) Simmer mixture for five to 10 minutes, till thickened slightly and heated completely through. Stir occasionally.

f) Smooth mixture in skillet. Sprinkle the cup of grated cheese over the top. Arrange tater tots in one layer, on the top. Sprinkle with remaining 1/2 cup of cheese.

g) Bake for 25-30 minutes. Cheese should be melted and tater tots should be browned. Remove from oven. Serve.

25 – Pineapple-Shrimp Quinoa Skillet

Makes 4 Servings

Cooking + Prep Time: 40 minutes

Ingredient List:

- 1/2 tsp. of cumin
- 1/2 lime, juice and zest only
- 1/2 tsp. of paprika
- 1 tbsp. of oil, olive

- 1 tsp. of garlic, minced
- 1/4 tsp. of salt, kosher
- 1 cup of water, filtered
- 1 pound of peeled, de-veined shrimp, raw
- 2/3 cup of diced green onions
- 1 1/2 cups of coconut milk, light
- 1/4 cup of diced cilantro + more to garnish
- 1 1/2 cups of quinoa, uncooked
- Optional: 1/2 cup of toasted coconut chips, unsweetened
- 2 cups of diced pineapple

Method:

a) In skillet on med-high, add garlic and oil.

b) Toss shrimp with salt, paprika and cumin. Sauté in oil for one or two minutes per side until cooked completely through and pink in color.

c) Remove shrimp from the pan. Set them aside.

d) Add quinoa. Toast for two to three minutes. You can add a little more oil, if you need to.

e) Add coconut milk, lime zest, green onion, pineapple and water to quinoa. Bring to boil. Cook over high heat for two to three minutes. Reduce heat to low.

Cover. Cook for 12-15 minutes and stir occasionally.

f) Three minutes before quinoa is done cooking, add shrimp back in, with lime juice.

g) Use coconut chips and cilantro to garnish. Serve promptly.

Skillet Desserts... Wait 'til you try them! Yum!

26 – Peach Cobbler, Skillet-Style

Makes 4-6 Servings

Cooking + Prep Time: 1 1/4 hours

Ingredient List:

For the peach filling

- 7 halved, sliced, pitted peaches
- 1/3 cup of sugar, granulated
- 1 pinch salt, kosher

- 2 tbsp. of butter, unsalted
- 1 1/2 tbsp. of corn starch
- 3/4 tsp. of vanilla extract, pure
- 1 tsp. of cinnamon, ground

For the topping

- 1 stick of cubed butter, unsalted
- 2 cups of flour, all-purpose
- 1 egg, large
- 1 1/2 tsp. of baking powder
- 1/4 tsp. of salt, kosher
- 1/2 cup of sugar, granulated
- 1/4 tsp. of baking soda
- 1/2 cup of buttermilk

Method:

a) Preheat oven to 375F.
b) Melt butter in oven-safe skillet on med. heat. Remove from heat when butter has melted.
c) To create the filling, add peaches to butter in skillet. Toss and coat well.

d) Whisk sugar, salt, corn starch and cinnamon together in small sized bowl. Add this to peaches. Toss to coat. Stir in vanilla extract.

e) To create the topping, pulse flour, salt, baking soda, baking powder and sugar in food processor. Add butter. Pulse till you have pea-sized pieces.

f) Transfer flour mixture to medium-sized bowl. Make well in middle. Add egg and buttermilk. Mix and combine well. Your mixture needs to crumble, like a streusel cake would. Crumble this topping over peaches in skillet evenly.

g) Transfer pan to 375F oven. Bake till topping turns golden brown in color. Filling should be bubbly. This usually takes between 35 and 40 minutes. Allow to cool for 10 minutes or a bit longer. Then slice and serve.

27 – Pineapple Upside-Down Skillet Cake

Makes 8 Servings

Cooking + Prep Time: 1 hour 20 minutes

Ingredient List:

- 1 cup of sugar, granulated

- 1 cup of buttermilk
- 1/2 tsp. of salt, kosher
- 2 cups of flour, all-purpose
- 8 de-stemmed maraschino cherries
- 8 tbsp. of melted butter, unsalted
- 1/2 tsp. of baking powder
- 1/2 cup of brown sugar, packed
- 2 eggs, large
- 8 x 1/2-inch thick slices of pineapple

Method:

a) Preheat the oven to 350F.

b) Pour 1/2 of butter in an oven-safe skillet. Swirl till sides and bottom of pan are coated with the butter.

c) Sprinkle the brown sugar over melted butter evenly in skillet. Place the slices of pineapple atop brown sugar.

d) Add a maraschino cherry in center of each slice of pineapple.

e) In medium bowl, combine the buttermilk, the rest of the butter, salt, baking powder, flour, sugar and eggs together. Whisk till combined well. Evenly pour over pineapple slices and the layer of brown sugar in skillet.

f) Place skillet in 350F oven for about 45 – 60 minutes. When inserted toothpick comes back clean, cake is done.

g) Remove skillet from oven. Allow it to sit for five to 10 minutes.

h) Place cake stand on the top of the skillet and flip carefully, so the cake comes out properly for an upside-down cake. Slice and serve.

28 – Skillet Brownies

Makes 5 Servings

Cooking + Prep Time: 50 minutes

Ingredient List:

- 1/4 cup + 1 tbsp. of flour, all-purpose
- 1/4 tsp. of salt, kosher
- 4 oz. + 1/2 cup of chocolate chips, semi-sweet
- 1 1/2 oz. of chopped chocolate, unsweetened
- 1 1/2 tsp. of vanilla extract, pure

- 1/2 cup of toffee bits
- 1/2 cup of butter, unsalted
- 1 tsp. of baking powder
- 1/2 cup of sugar, granulated
- 2 eggs, large

Method:

a) Preheat oven to 350F.

b) In large sized bowl above simmering water, melt the unsweetened chocolate and chocolate chips until their texture is smooth. Set them aside to cool for 12-15 minutes or so.

c) Stir eggs, sugar and vanilla together in another large bowl. Stir chocolate mixture into egg mixture till combined well.

d) Sift 1/4 cup flour, salt and baking powder together in medium sized bowl. Add to chocolate mixture. Stir till barely combined.

e) In medium sized bowl, toss remaining 1/2 cup chocolate chips, along with 1 tbsp. flour and toffee bits together. Fold into chocolate mixture.

f) Divide batter in five small oven-safe skillets. Place skillets on cookie sheet. Put in oven and bake them for 20-30 minutes. Be careful that you don't overbake them.

g) Remove skillets from oven. You can top the skillet brownies with toffee bits, ice cream or hot fudge, if you like. Serve.

29 – Skillet Apple Pie

Makes 8-10 Servings

Cooking + Prep Time: 2 hours

Ingredient List:

- 1 tsp. of cinnamon, ground
- 2 lbs. of Granny Smith apples
- 1 large egg white
- For serving: Ice cream
- 2 tbsp. of sugar, granulated

- 2 lbs. of Braeburn apples
- 1 pkg. of 2 pie crusts, refrigerated
- 1 cup of brown sugar, light, packed firmly
- 3/4 cup of sugar, granulated
- 1/2 cup of butter, unsalted2 tbsp. of sugar, granulated

Method:

a) Preheat the oven to 350F.

b) Peel the apples. Cut them into wedges about 1/2" thick. Toss the apples with granulated sugar and cinnamon.

c) Melt the butter in an oven-safe skillet on med. heat. Add the brown sugar. Stir constantly while cooking, for a couple minutes, till all sugar has dissolved. Remove pan from the stove top burner. Place one pie crust in the skillet on top of the brown sugar mixture.

d) Spoon the apple mixture over the pie crust. Top with the second pie crust. Whisk the egg till it foams. Brush top pie crust with egg white. Sprinkle with 2 tbsp. of sugar. Then cut several slits in the top crust for escaping steam.

e) Bake for one hour to one hour 10 minutes at 350F. It should be bubbly and golden brown. Cool on wire rack for 1/2 hour. Serve with ice cream, as desired.

30 – Skillet Berry Cake

Makes 8 Servings

Cooking + Prep Time: 55 minutes

Ingredient List:

- 1/2 cup of sugar, brown
- 3 tbsp. of flour, all-purpose
- 1 tbsp. of softened butter
- 1/4 tsp. of baking soda
- 1/2 cup of buttermilk, low-fat
- For the topping

- 3/4 cup of sugar, granulated
- 1 egg, large
- 1/2 tsp. of cinnamon, ground
- 1 cup of pastry flour, whole-wheat
- 1/2 cup each of raspberries, sliced strawberries and blueberries
- 1/2 tsp. of baking powder
- 1/4 tsp. of salt, kosher
- 4 tbsp. of softened butter, unsalted

Method:

a) Preheat oven to 375F.

b) Whisk baking soda, salt, baking powder and flour together in small sized bowl. Set it aside.

c) Beat sugar and butter till fluffy with electric mixer. Add egg. Mix and combine.

d) Add flour slowly, followed by some of the buttermilk, then some more flour. Scrape this batter into cooking-sprayed skillet. Spread better to edges. Dot top of batter with assorted berries.

e) In a separate bowl, mix topping ingredients together. Sprinkle over berries.

f) Place skillet in your oven. Bake for 1/2 hour or so, till it starts browning and inserted toothpick comes back clean. Remove from oven. Serve warm.

Printed in Great Britain
by Amazon

85175470R00051